CAA Award for Poetry

Gerald Lampert Memorial Prize Finalist

Dorothy Livesay Poetry Prize Finalist

"Elise Partridge, whose *Chameleon Hours* records the author's near brush with death, [offers] both a benevolent and a meaningful response to the threat of extinction. Mostly, Partridge records her horror obliquely and with considerable humour."
— Patrick Warner, *Riddlefence*

"A fully formed voice speaks in these poems that invite us to share their closely observed particulars — a hospitable voice, full of intelligence, good humour, candour, engagement. Each poem commands attention. Exemplary."
— Robyn Sarah, *National Post*

"First rate . . . a true heir of Elizabeth Bishop."
— James Pollock, *poetryreviews.ca*

"Partridge's adjectives bristle with life from page one . . . [she] has a knack for creating resonating, symbolic, and yet gently strange images."
— Jana Prikryl, *Books in Canada*

"Reading [Partridge's work], I find myself marvelling at the luck of each person, place, thing, or circumstance, to have Elise Partridge's exquisite and precise attention. And how lucky we are to get to listen in as she offers each of them her flawless ear."
— Jacqueline Osherow

"Elise Partridge brings the most mundane moments vividly to life."
— *Vancouver Sun*

"Elise Partridge's *Chame'* received on both sides of observed, meaningful, an to make passionate art fr and the possibility of losi
— Barbara Myers, *Arc*

ges
ness

T0150975

THE EXILES' GALLERY

ELISE PARTRIDGE

ANANSI

This edition published in 2015 by
House of Anansi Press Inc.
110 Spadina Avenue, Suite 801
Toronto, ON, M5V 2K4
Tel. 416-363-4343, Fax 416-363-1017
www.houseofanansi.com

Distributed in Canada by
HarperCollins Canada Ltd.
1995 Markham Road
Scarborough, ON, M1B 5M8
Toll free tel. 1-800-387-0117

Distributed in the United States by
Publishers Group West
1700 Fourth Street
Berkeley, CA, 94710
Toll free tel. 1-800-788-3123

House of Anansi Press is committed to protecting our natural environment.
As part of our efforts, the interior of this book is printed on paper made from
second-growth forests and is acid-free.

19 18 17 16 15   1 2 3 4 5

Library and Archives Canada Cataloguing in Publication
Partridge, Elise, author
The exiles' gallery / Elise Partridge.
Poems.
Issued in print and electronic formats.
ISBN 978-1-77089-980-3 (bound).—ISBN 978-1-77089-979-7 (pbk.).—
ISBN 978-1-77089-981-0 (pdf)
I. Title.
PS8581.A7665E95 2015   C811'.6   C2014-908363-7
C2014-908364-5

Library of Congres Control Number: 2014953192

Cover design: Brian Morgan
Text design: Alysia Shewchuk
Typesetting: Brian Morgan

*We acknowledge for their financial support of our publishing program
the Canada Council for the Arts, the Ontario Arts Council, and the Government of
Canada through the Canada Book Fund.*

Printed and bound in Canada

With thanks to

*Christopher, Derry,
Diane, Kenneth,
Robert, Robert,
and Ruth*

And, as always, to Steve
Happy We

CONTENTS

IV

I CAN'T EXPLAIN how Elise Partridge's poems achieve their clear outlines and deep textures. At certain moments an athlete or dancer, executing a familiar move, can seem somehow a little less affected by gravity or time. For me, these poems often reach that kind of distinction, with lucidity reaching a new, unanticipated level of brightness.

For example, in a poem entitled "Citydwellers" some airshaft pigeons evoke the people whose windows share that same space. The two kinds of citydwellers in their vertical habitat: a straightforward equivalent of a thrown ball or a dancer's leap. It's the execution that distinguishes the writing as it leaps beyond mere competence, to something sharper:

Under air conditioners' juts,
they nap on tilting ledges,
these pairs that mate for life.
The shimmer they were born with —
the rainbow covenant each wears —
grants no privilege,

nor does it offer anything
to other creatures in their pens
around the blackened shaft:
the man crooning to
a child, the kerchiefed widow
sweeping her railroad kitchen.

The vignette is quotidian, the setting is familiar — but the twelve-line passage is remarkably alive. It is even, though unshowy, kind of daring: "creatures" might feel too bold or corny if it weren't supported by the Biblical "rainbow covenant." "Covenant" and "creature," like "privilege," contrast with, and lighten, the earthbound main key of crammed juts, tilting ledges, the blackened shaft, and the fretting child. The powers of eye and ear create an urgent reality.

A much different poem, "Last Days," concentrates on an extreme situation, with the urgency inherent: a young woman, pregnant and with cancer, struggles to live long enough for her child's birth. Here, those same gifts of observation and cadence master the awful drama:

My friend, you wouldn't lie down.
Your wandering IV pole
glided with you, loyal, rattling
on frantic circuits;
crisp pillows didn't tempt;
round, around, around, guppies

cruised the lobby tank,
flickering sunrise-slivers
all guts, mouths urging, urging;
tube-lights buzzed like bees
over your pale shoulders;
you wadded your pink gown, yanked

on crimson sweats . . .

The IV apparatus, the fish, the clashing colours, "wadded" cloth, skin, the hospital itself tank-like, all deftly vivid, are put in their place by the refrain of "round, around, around." The element of song tempers the pathos and memorializes the purposeful effort. In another iteration:

scout in a cornered valley,
you looped your length of ground
as cancer hurtled to break

the bones that kept you pacing,
carrying your handsbreadth girl
(five-month spindle Buddha,
her brain's coral byways
travelled by your voice);
round, around, around, you

duelled to stay alive until
she could be born.

In this book, the force of judgment in art — in this example the taste to emphasize the images evoked by the refrain, the economy of "her brain's coral byways" and "handsbreadth girl" — becomes the same thing as moral judgment: the taste to admire the young woman's determination just enough, and in just the right way, so that the admiration doesn't lapse into admiring itself, or courting the reader's esteem.

In other words, Partridge keeps her eye on the facts, enabling impressive actions of heart and mind like "Citydwellers" and "Last Days." But it would be wrong to leave out another element in this book: a capacity for yearning, a sense of the otherworldly. A memorable moment of that kind is in the closing lines of "Parish Dance." The girl, in early adolescence, wanders away from the awkward dance, and with Shakespeare's *Romeo and Juliet* in her mind looks up at the stars. In a characteristic Partridge moment, the images are celestial and mundane, dreamy and real, ordinary and ardent:

As the bored band lurched into another tune,
I wandered through the darkling parking lot.
"Lady, by yonder blessèd moon I vow —"
All I could see was Armstrong
bounding across its crust,
boldly gone;
Shepard tapping his Titleist into dust.
Crossed stars!
Venus obscured. . . .
And the Rover's shiny sled
maneuvering light wheels,
bewildered, dogged, lone,
assessing Mars.

More like the assessing, shiny, and resourceful Rover than the heroic, golfing astronauts, this aspiring, understated imagination goes far, with a quiet assurance of vision.

— *Robert Pinsky*

THE EXILES' GALLERY

I

One ancient bayside city in a balmy palette:
peach façades, a fuchsia door,
boys flipping open a creel.
Five shirts take their ease on a jigging clothesline,
white sleeves buoyant and secure.

Virgil was schooled here,
just beyond this etching.
How hard, the next pastel suggests, to leave any city
that invented opera buffa,
not to mention the mandolin.

Three hallway maps immortalize
hamlets in baroque fonts.
Trees neat as a row of asterisks
fleck a diagrammed bosque.
Mountains look cozy as tents

ringing another town, settled in shuttles
of Celts, Slavs, Germans —
Paleo-trench to *oppidum* to stockade;
its Bohemia became renowned
as a magicians' haven.

But Nero summered in one city,
shelling unroofed two more;
that bosque gardener's son
couldn't rise (and who even thought of
the mapmaker's daughter?),

.

coins weren't worth bottlecaps,
plague deployed rat-tailed crews,
farms shrivelled with famine, and streets
where prayer-shawls had fluttered three hundred years
were cleared of Jews.

Just one painting by an amateur:
pads of cumuli;
heeling on cobalt waves, a brown skiff.
Those watching it tilt, weeping,
can't catch the voyager's eye —

a girl in black — thin arms —
gazes toward no sign of land.
Her face is turned away;
she grips a jolting tiller
in her too-small hand.

BIOGRAPHY

I woke cold and wet on a hill,
was handed vouchers to mazes.

Wished I could bury myself
in a sugarbowl,
safe from the giants' rage
down my porcelain well.

A storm in a raspberry's hollow,
at school I studied balking.

Diploma'd, was granted interviews
but my
credentials were birdscratched runes.

Work: I was shrunk
to a poppyseed
down slick microchip aisles.
I slept in the drawers
of a banker's file.

Love, opening vistas?
At first; then savannahs
receded, I was stranded
in a varnished diorama —
peeling cumuli,
popcorn ceiling —
ogled by a guard.

Found myself in the city,
a strand on a barbershop floor.

DOMINION
Vancouver, British Columbia

Under the grackles' bridge
two azure pennants snap —
a faded turret's luffing
on a child's backyard tent.
This runnel-moat Windsor's
thane gropes at sunrise
through frayed plastic flaps.

The Fairmont Estates are rising
"for luxury connoisseurs"
 north of his scrounged fief.
"Wolf Ranges. Three Gated Stalls."
Nailguns tack, tack, tacking.
Dodging the fusillade,
the silver-haired seigneur

steps out in nylon hauberk.
He sifts a treasure-midden's
clanking, needled bin,
bags two nickel grails;
pop dribbles through his fingers
down his sleeves. He limps
toward glass pavilions,

winces; wilts on a curb;
cradles his chapping heel.
Above him, arithmancers
assess each offshore take.
Back at Fairmont's scaffold,

delivery men unwrap
freezers of burnished steel,

snug insulation-rolls;
concrete pits keep drying.
The Knight of the Rusting Cart
creaks back by dusk
when the corner toy-store
takes down its Merlin flag.
His pennants go on flying.

MY LAST DUCHESS (THE MANSERVANT)

I sailed from England with her, when the Lords
settled the dowry — I got room and board
at the Duke's castle. Found it quite grim
at first — can't say I ever liked him,
but you couldn't not like her. She had a spark,
galloping that mule to the edge of the park
till the Duke had it put down. He'd say,
"What will you do with yourself today
while I'm out hunting, my silly little wren?"
— things like that. He'd ride off with his men.
He had her portrait painted, but nearly sacked
the monk who did it — didn't ask him back
even when it was unveiled. She was lonely,
homesick — too young. She talked a lot with me.
Once the Duke barged in and grabbed her wrist
and hauled her down the gallery, where he kissed
her, hard. He didn't know I saw her wince.
One night I heard him rage when a German prince
made her laugh: she'd dropped a silver cup,
bowed to thank the prince when he picked it up.
My last week there, I didn't feel my best,
and she seemed blue; she gave me leave to rest
each afternoon. Was it the sudden heat,
she wondered: "They're running you off your feet.
They ask too much." She made us want to please.
That evening, I remember, we caught a breeze
under the cherries. Once she'd strolled a while
I cut a spray for her. She bowed, then smiled.

He can see miles of uptown suites
from his Pollock office chair (gouged, tilting,
a dumpster rescue wheeled late at night).
Like a CEO hurled there by a twister,
he swivels, as if mulling bonuses —
this percent for whom? For him, what hoard?
— greenbacks to blow like leaves along the streets

below the Exchange's flag.
Twenty billion were shaken down last year.
"Not from my Sherwood Forest,"
he mutters. On Fifth, he huddles deeper
near his entrance to the Park
(a titan's given its acres a hundred million),
swathed in a gray mummy-bag,

querying its mottled sleeve;
down the block, the varnished *boiserie*
of the coke-magnate mansion's gallery
he visited once, on a class trip
with his P.S. across the river.
Ruddy Dutch merchants; a Sèvres teacup;
a king glaring above his hammered greaves

near panelled, dimpled whimsies by Boucher
for Mrs. Frick's boudoir — rosy children
(commissioned by a mistress at Versailles)
practicing the arts. Dancing, painting,
poetry; one boy tweets on a recorder.

He sees these children hurried to their lessons,
the miniature violins every day

bustled past the reservoir
after school. There, one icy night,
he argued until dawn with an owl.
You have not learned your lessons,
the owl said. They tussled over a sparkler;
the beak dangled it; gaped —
the black water gulped it, his lucky star.

But he'll stay here, with his securities,
in the February dusk: the chair, the bag,
the white dog in the tartan vest who sniffs him
every Sunday, the owners strolling
toward brassy lobbies paced by greatcoat guards.
His ears ache. Next fall he will accept
some small donations from these golden trees.

ASTROLABE

1.
As he had sent his astrolabe and his other modest baggage
over the river with the caravan,
he had to follow.

2.
In his drawing-room stood the chest containing
all his instruments and papers from the expedition.

3.
He would often take his old astrolabe and wander over
    the marshes.

When the lines all ran together,
he had to put his mapping pen aside.

4.
As he had sent his astrolabe and his other modest baggage
over the river with the caravan,
she had to follow.

6.
She submitted a request to be given the vacant post of clerk.

Her reports were rare and brief.

I stand, legs astride, a colossus —
or dancer in fifth position, wide *port de bras.*
Polymorph strayed into English,

sometimes pronounced like Americans' *z,*
in French I'm often silent; in Pirahã the glottal stop;
a fricative in Somali.

Vector, Cartesian axis,
chromosome, bowling-strike. Pirate-map cynosure;
at a letter's close, a kiss.

I do plebeian duty in tic tac toe,
range marble façades. Paired with *y,* I dodge —
variable incognito.

I lend myself to comets of cryptic orbit,
ally with rays that pierce time's edge.
I'm default sci-fi planets.

In my Roman hours,
I was ten. — Later, the name of millions:
those never granted an alphabet's power.

CO-EDUCATION

He scowls in his bat-sleeve gown
at girls crossing Front Court
(only dons can walk on the grass).
His bedder in her frayed apron
hauls buckets the long way around.

LEGACIES

She is handsome, she is pretty,
She is the belle of Belfast City
— Ulster folk song

Her father groomed rich men's roses,
then sailed his family west
— in the New World they could rise.
She married in a rose cloche.

For weekly strolls to market
she put on white gloves, a hat;
charms — a tiger dangling;
a rose-and-silver heart.

Shine, shine, shine, shine,
her copper pans; her floors
glazed like honey; the tray
with initials twined.

Her husband took the wheel
(she didn't learn to drive).
Fifty years later, he dozed
wasting on her rose chenille,

an effigy, two months, eight —
how could he leave her now?
How could she stay behind?
Months after they waked her knight,

．

she said goodbye, in gibberish.
To her son she left her land,
to her daughter, silver, charms,
and the rose Coalport dish.

EMIGRÉS

We swing the ax down on the fraying rope
that ties us to your dock,
that cramped isle you ruled where no girl spoke
her mind. You, benighted queen,
gave your land to sons and left your daughters
barely a lean-to thatched with shredding fronds.
Now we welcome the widening water.

FOR A WOMAN BORN IN THE 1930s

Her inner itineraries —
trails hacked by love and need —
were recorded in runes
that faded. Other
adventures foundered
on this sugarbowl's dunes.

If she might have been launched
in one of these vessels —
helped to embark in the milk-glass dish
or swerve upriver — to study chinooks? —
in that etched kayak she heaped
with homemade relish.

Hoist her white leather valise,
a gift when she was eighteen —
its aura of vista and risk,
initials gold by the tortoise handle.
Nudge the brass locks: they pop,
untarnished, brisk.

DOMESTIC INTERIOR:
CHILD WATCHING MOTHER

Chapped hands sift greasy suds.
She can't make rent. Quietly,
she's crying again.

Vessels tip in the rack.
Each night I watch her eyes
to make sure they keep drying.

WALTZING

I can see just so much
from my studio flat
through the slanting snow:
my neighbour sweeps his daughter
around their condo
in off-kilter, three-
quarter time: whisk,
promenade, slow dip —
she must be riding his toes —
while his wife whirls their son
to Benny Goodman,
or looping bluegrass fiddles.

The last time my parents waltzed:
their wedding day.
After she flung her violets,
he tossed a champagne flute.
"I hated him doing that."
Wasn't it exciting,
I asked once. She frowned.
"I wanted it over with."
As they duck sparse confetti
in this gray shot,
knowing how it ended,
I hold my breath.

My neighbour's daughter claps
as they lurch right
again, by the rumpled
couch; her mother

can't stop grinning.
The girl stumbles, her father
swoops her up to
the rafters, the son
swats a balloon.
They flick off the ceiling bulb,
conga out of sight
to their inaudible tune.

TREE

The farmer looked bent
as scrub-pines
stunted by gales,
hands splotched with oil
from the sputtering truck.
His son showed me the foal
— the forehead's star —
then a flowering plum.
"I got that for my dad."
His father glanced away.
"You didn't plant it well."
At dusk I saw the boy
hurl plums at the corral.

We veered in anxious circles,
then gobbled pretzels.
I queried partners as my mom proposed.
"What subjects do you like?" "Do you play sports?"
"Wrestling," said Joe. Grinning — "I pulled my groin."
What is a groin? I wondered. *Isn't it —?*
I'd look it up.
I watched cola flatten in my cup.

That morning I'd been lightning at the blackboard,
relished the nimble pairing of new words.
In woodworking I'd roughed out a canoe.

As the bored band lurched into another tune,
I wandered through the darkling parking lot.
"Lady, by yonder blessèd moon I vow —"
All I could see was Armstrong
bounding across its crust,
boldly gone;
Shepard tapping his Titleist into dust.
Crossed stars!
Venus obscured. . . .
And a Rover's shiny sled
maneuvering light wheels,
bewildered, dogged, lone,
assessing Mars.

METH

You strode into the bar
dressed up like death —
black jacket, cap, boots —
you hadn't slept for days
plummeting from a high, about
to crash, blazing.
We said, "Please take care."
You stiffened, fists clenched,
as if you'd take it as a dare
to risk what you had left.

Night after night after night, he couldn't sleep.
In the room next door, he'd mutter Latin verse,
or pace the house till dawn, then trudge the beach
with undecided terns. He asked us all
to take care not to step where plovers' eggs
lay tucked in slipping dunes. "A scholar!" scoffed
my father. "Head in the clouds!"
                                                    Mornings,
I'd scrub the breakfast dishes, swipe a rag
over Doulton flounces, bustles, and bows,
squirt polish on the toes of table-legs
and, once each had been inspected, sprawl
to tan, flipping through romance novels.
Weekends, my brothers and I blasted ducks
in boardwalk shooting galleries, or slapped down bids
for Ventnor on our scarred Monopoly board.
One day my uncle found me at the clothesline
hanging my brothers' socks. "Bonjour. Ça va?"
He knew I took French at school. "Voila,
un grand mouchoir!" "Oui," I murmured, shy.
"'Le bateau ivre,'" he muttered toward the speedboat
slapping the bay. Had I ever heard, he asked,
of Marie de France — how in one of her tales
a boat sails you off to love the minute you board?
I shook my head. "I'd skip the Cartland, and try her."
Two days later he sought me out again,
and as we fished damp shirts from the laundry tub,
he'd pass me with each clothespin a *bon mot*.
Once when I was hosing out the crab-trap,
he told me how Gérard de Nerval

had strolled a lobster through Paris, on a leash.
"What do you want to do with your good brain?"
he asked one blistering day. I shrugged; blushed.
In August, "'our summer made her light escape,'"
he said, "and I should too"— he left to teach.
"Write me whenever you can about what you read."
He gave me a list, told me to follow my nose.
Jane Eyre; the Bennet sisters; Marianne Moore;
The Portrait of a Lady; *Silent Spring*—
I rushed to write him; he always wrote right back.
When Father Stodd said women couldn't be priests,
he sent me a wry postcard of Voltaire.
One day a bulky book of poems arrived,
my first. "Read these aloud. Try to write a poem."

You drifted from the family and died young.
What were you thinking, nights you stayed awake?
Sit with me on the porch, we'll talk till dawn;
quote me all you know of Virgil's eclogues —
the lonely shepherd's protest; the tended vine.

THEN

"Palm readings by the pair" —
fortunes in the city!
Stale patchouli whiffs,
a spidery chandelier;
gold at her turtle throat.
Her pilling shawl was fringed
with foggy opal tears.

She gripped our hands in hers
and squinted. She saw
glittering midnight bridges,
riddles tucked in gourds;
faces with flowing beards
that meant us only good;
a pair of knightly pledges

secured by ring and keys.
She said a brusque farewell,
lowered kohl-streaked lids.
Linking arms, we strode
back to our avenues,
jaunty, just nineteen,
to troll like rowdy gods.

Twelve years old, we squeeze hip to hip
for the class photo
in blue-lettered caps.
Newspapers have lent our schoolwork
hopeful facts

on curing bolting cancers,
rescuing bleached reefs,
regrafting a grain
that could feed a continent,
fast-forward jaunts to the moon.

Sin at our age
means arriving late
for roll-call. We already know the victories
of coaxing kites out of elms,
solving for y.

We haven't met our stark scaffold
in the school lab —
cartilage like dried apricot
linking sprung staves
that had sheltered a heart.

Tragedies are still sequestered
in great-aunts' silences
and uncut books.
None of us believe in Robespierres
of mere luck;

we can't imagine
our seedling gifts
topping at sprout,
or tangling ourselves beyond surfacing
in ghost-nets;

foresee our caches of memories
emptied at death
like an old barn
so careless of what it kept
it tossed its roof to a storm.

The girl who lost her mind —
no one can find her now —
grins from row four.
She always came first in hurdles,
seven straight years.

STRAWBERRY CUTTINGS

After a month away, we're greeted
by a blackening shock — stalks
drooping from a butter tub
to our welcome-mat's ruff.
I grip a nub, brusque as a thorn,
that dissolves to puffs.

A gift from a friend? But who?
That evening, a neighbour knocks.
"I thought you should know —
Joan had another attack —
the worst of all.
She killed herself last week."

Joan, who each Friday strode
to the corner bodega
for kibbles and day-old bread,
pausing sometimes to chat
cautiously, wittily
under her creased sunhat,

about her newest library haul —
Woolf, Berryman, John Clare, Blake. . . .
We'd sealed her leaking porch sill
with a dribble of caulk,
once boarded her cat,
flipped blizzard drifts from the sidewalk

she'd lined with strawberries,
rue, sage. She'd had to quit nursing

as the voices kept breaking in —
"I've never known when they'd leave."
Her berry-slip tucked below
our fortunate eaves

must have earned barely a spatter,
waiting for our return.
I curl it into the compost
with black-flecked hands,
which could perhaps have saved this
with a half-pint watering can.

RETURN

Was it always trite,
this landscape, pleading
to be abandoned?

Board game
with peeling
corners to shove

on a closet shelf,
its faded
players scattered? Here

stands the old school,
its serial ordeals
mere hopscotch choices;

those blackboards loomed
like wailing walls
where I prayed

to remember primes —
for giants
in pilling cardigans.

Home: bricks
and a yard,
shivering ivy.

.

If I sat there
for dinner now,
the chandelier's prongs

would snag in my hair,
my huge foot
frighten the cat.

Two trees clutch
gnawed plums
in wizened fingers.

The queen
begs to sell
me quinces,

the king's
a carter hobbling
down the road;

they want
me to take their hands —
but it's just moss

hanging like
sleeves, and the trill
of wrens.

CITYDWELLERS

The pigeons are trilling — buttery contralto notes —
in this airshaft-kingdom's chute
with one slick trunk, a dented pipe.
The scraps of gray or blue above
sometimes allow a glimpse
of a cloud's casual route.

Under air conditioners' juts,
they nap on tilting ledges,
these pairs that mate for life.
The shimmer they were born with —
the rainbow covenant each wears —
grants no privilege,

nor does it offer anything
to other creatures in their pens
around the blackened shaft:
the man crooning to
a child, the kerchiefed widow
sweeping her railroad kitchen.

They all hear, from the shaft's sunless floor,
the super clinking cans
he fishes from the trash
each day in dripping sacks.
These concerts continue all night,
played by binners' hands

on other streets throughout the city —
where busboys heft and lower silver kegs

to four-star cellars, and deliverymen
with pizzas strapped to bikes careen
past town-cars. An office cleaner,
run off aching legs,

tunnels under the moat (three changes)
to the bedroom in a borough
she shares with four; her neighbour
starts the dishes at 3 a.m.,
fingers stiff from scouring pop off seats
at midnight shows

after her BK shift. So many with their backs
against cracked walls —
ordinary, extraordinary nesters, tenders
to princes and their suites. Can
any luck hold up, or change for good,
when the New Year's pure flakes begin to fall?

II

No mountain deities
that flattered cows
or flash-froze girls into trees.

Cross-species confabs in lairs —
a landscape giddy with fellowship.
Dormice groomed a bear.

And each crop a loyal perennial.
That infinite stash of pippins,
cores shied over a wall!

Aligned by a keyboard
into parade-band precisions,
or squeezed and ballooned
— addled-looking
as in drunken wedding-shots —
from blunting tips of crayons.

They change partners nimbly
for human callers,
shape-shift between
capital and lowercase.

Thickly Gothic, honed Danish-modern,
they'll tilt for the italic wand,
deepen haberdashery
when summoned to be "bold."

One-liners, testaments,
inventories, chants,
condolences, mattress labels,
they keep flocking to Anonymous's hand,
assembling without reproach
even for those who can't spell.

In Babel, they also lay down and wept.

Whacked through nights, a pinball dribbled down a hole.

Sourdough starter, pale, that didn't rise.

Announcement at intermission, *La Bohème.*

Tunnelled hurriedly through twenty-two acres.

Smelting spark whisked through a ceiling slit.

Five a.m. wandering wisp of laundromat steam.

Mud.
Skies over Round Top shift,
      gray, gray-blue.
             Red
                    splatters wheat, fresh peaches.

Union
crouched on a front porch, Rebels in back,
blast through velveteen drapes
on Baltimore Street.

                  Lilypads brimming blood.

Tweedle, tump-tump,
tweedle — Army bands.

One family nurses pickets from the Potomac.
(When that river ran low, Northern
and Southern soldiers, from opposite
banks, had waded joking, parleying for tobacco.)

A girl lugs for burial legs and hands.

COLLATERAL DAMAGE

Anything vertical to the horizon
wants to fall.
No: we want to stay
upright; our shear-walls

resist the load of wind.
Don't we stand on solid
shoring? All our valuables sheltered —
affections; a brain. . . .

One floor of a building collapses
to about a foot of debris.
Tall, slender structures
would rather topple like trees.

(The bodies, laid out in rows;
the nests, in the crushed boughs.)

We phoned in our votes
on key issues; young interns,
politely, made a note. Last spring we glimpsed
an aide from our own state, when our bus tour
gawked at the White House gate.

On Primary Day,
wind blew one candidate's speech
into the bay. The loudspeakers blared blurrily
all during the rally; red, white and blue
balloons drifted off up an alley.

That fall we peered into the set
at the poised incumbent,
tracked beads of sweat stippling the challenger's lip
as he denied indiscretions, mikes bobbing,
spokespeople shouting "No more questions!"

At the Inaugural,
high-school fifes tootled off
sharpshooter-defended walls; agents glowered.
When the motorcade finally passed, we snapped a dim hand
waving behind black glass.

PLACARD AT THE LOS ANGELES
EXCAVATION SITE, 5002 A.D.

These concrete pits at the rear of their dwellings
may have been used for cooking purposes:
charred grates and aluminum cans nearby
are consistent with feasts they called "barbecues."
The pits were constructed to receive bright sun,
which we think they worshipped as a deity.
Patterns of tiles arranged around the edge
may have shown off the possessors' wealth.

Some believe the pits were used for ritual games,
others conjecture for human sacrifice:
their society was known for violence,
judging by the number of skeletons unearthed
with bullet trauma to ribs or skull.
Some pits have springboards where we think priests stood,
rousing spectators with now-lost chants.
The drains at the bottom might have caught blood.

THOREAUVIAN

At the racetrack,
he scoured the tip-sheet
to bet on the scorned filly.

The day the CEO visited,
he kept his appointment
with a forsythia.

He tithed his salary,
every other year,
to an unlucky aunt.

In the museum
of war heroes,
he noted the helmets' plumes.

— Truces that never occurred,
signed by dignitaries
in Great-Hall ceremonies
wearing their conjured eras' odd chapeaux
by balustrades looped with garlands.
Zinnias of parachute
dimensions; lime-scented squids;
cities with fields
for roofs. . . .

The contradictory analogue
to *World Books, Britannicas* — where
someone in a glaring lab
is congratulated on breakthroughs
whose unforeseeable application
will result in a billion graves.

The *I. E.* wouldn't need entries
on civilizations recorded
with "not much is known,"
on peoples remembered by
unstrung beads,
languages whose idioms ghosted away
like smoke,
epics condensed
to crusaders' ash.

Nor will it need to lament
antennae ferning a stone,
the snail's turret

tucked only in specimen drawers,
that island swallow last glimpsed
in a colonist's cat's jaws.

It would skimp
on the descent of kings
or a towering GNP,
in favour of long bios
of mothers who walked miles for water,
a farmer who shared his well.

LITANY

*Extinction can be documented only for species known to have
existed in the first place — and only when an observer has noted
their passing. Because at most only 10% of the species suspected
to be living on earth have been identified, it is certain that many
more species have become extinct in the past than are listed here.*
— Museum of Natural History, New York

Luna County Globemallow
    Tombigbee Moccasin Shell
Ascension Flightless Crake
    Rodrigues Little Owl

Brazilian Diving Beetle
    Reunion Solitaire
Mt. Diablo Buckwheat
    Thismia; Orkney Char

Shasta River Mariposa
    Umbilical Pebble Snail
Robust Burrowing Mayfly
    Great Auk; Red Gazelle

Dobson's Painted Bat
    Sloth Lemur; Stumptooth Minnow
Mauritius Night Heron
    O'ahu 'O'o

Pig-Footed Bandicoot
    Xerxes Blue Butterfly

St. Helena Giant Earwig
    Parras Pupfish; Franklin Tree

Ilin Cloudrunner Rat
    Maine, Old Veteran Rush
Yellow Kite Swallowtail
    Pt. Reyes Indian Paintbrush

Guadalupe Caracara
    Long-Nosed Island Shrew
New Providence Hummingbird
    Broad-Faced Potoroo

Cerulean Paradise Flycatcher
    Whipple's Monkey-Flower
Farwell's Blue-Eyed Lovegrass
    Sugarspoon; Phantom Shiner.

If they had straightened, not veered,
if they'd caught the night ferry.
If the Consul's clerk had replied,
if west-running tracks had cleared.

If she'd taken the hallway stairs.
If he hadn't missed the warning
while he whistled at tea.
If they'd walked home late from the fair.

III

There's one tied to a fence
by a rancher yearning for shade.
Lashed to a mall's arch,
two shift dolorous
haunches, chained elephants.

Not just bits of scenery
towed by deity-fingers
deft, abstracted as typists',
their management praised
in Wesleyan homilies —

but flocks nabbed for sets
by producers, tugged
down the coast, Burbanked
for cameos, wrangled
to shroud a turret.

A cloud's birthright: to drift.
But they'd be baled, surely —
sweatshop bolsters on pallets;
or bartered, resort-backlog
dragged over ski-lifts;

parade-effigies corralled
toward sooty boulevards;
stockpiled by Defense,
crammed into silos
for a hurricane arsenal.

If hoarded for personal grief
or rich children's kites,
perhaps a grassroots co-op
could assemble thousands
for launching — relief

during tar-melt Julys
to cool barrio alleys,
stack above parched corn,
refresh a threatened pampa's
bellwether fly.

Here, one is the only décor
snagged by the truck-stop
where the waitress pauses,
admiring its mauves
from a booth by the door

as she dabs at a mustard smear.
When her shift ends,
she strides through the parking lot
and snips its soiled tether
with the night cook's shears.

FATES

That baby dying of measles
for lack of vaccine;
or this one, of dehydration
an eight-cent pill might have cured?

Atropos:
My fingers, my whole hand aches.
I'm blamed for losses,
though we work in tandem.
New shears each week —
I don't get much of a break,
can't be bothered with tears.

Lachesis:
I'm doomed to fulfill
my executive role;
not an hour of relief.
But one can't expect good luck
— isn't everything random?

Clotho:
I was granted two remedies
for grief:
to watch threads bulk on the spindle;
to hum to the hum of my wheel.

HUMMINGBIRD KOAN
for Barbara Nickel

Mountainpeak

hush.

Grove
like a
revelation-booth.

        Wish-rush of pines,
        wish-rush —

I wait for truth
to descend like a mitre.

    (Elliptical scrabble.
            Chipmunks?)

Dzzz dzzz dzzz —
        green-and-radishy flashing

                Glean   glean   glean

They couldn't give it away, I guess,
so left it beside the road,
where, obdurate, it warps.
No gnawed pencils now, no fingers drumming,
just catkin loads

floating across this escritoire,
nailed after Oberon's band
skewed Snug and Quince's vision —
an improv, overnight effort
planed with a moonstruck hand,

its driftwood-assortment legs
unanswerable as a colt's.
Scrap-yard rescue, no single
edge flush — three fraying planks,
three widths, burled with gunk-smeared bolts.

Not for a codicil flourish
or crisp blueprint. No pressed-wood-and-glue,
but a landing-strip for particulars
of uncertain provenance —
not a board true, for the true.

Bulbous, chromed like a Studebaker;
fifty years old, like the house;
only one burner still lit —
even unwatched pots wouldn't boil.
Offhand advice said junk it.
But not our friend Klaus.

Clanking, he leapt from his truck,
cranked the stove's snowy hood;
peered into glass-fuse orbs.
Gingerroot thumbs nudged coils.
With falcon-beak pliers, he stirred
black-lava reaches of crud,

knit frizzing wire. He eased
the range sideways, humming,
draped copper around new bolts,
strands over a child's ear;
tapped; squinted; hovered —
ruddying, a quartet of suns.

Klaus shook his head
at our cheque, patted the stove's
chipped door. "Bake me two stollen."
With your labour of double love
you will give us hundreds,
and all you ask is two loaves.

Canadian, American, First Nations,
they posed at
a Simcoe farm
with mothers, fathers, kids,
Rick's chicken-hypnotist uncle
and blues-troubadour clan.

No acid-trip liner
for this debut. Through snowbound
sessions in a rented basement
they'd syncopate breaks
— however many takes it took.
Ignoring cashbag diviners,

they'd spend an hour on pairs
of arpeggios, weeks on
live tracks — wiring bridges,
rechannelling grooves, Garth
smoking soprano riffs
like wraiths up a D-scale stair.

Ten years on the road, played
Winnipeg to Arkansas,
a tin shed with three brawlers.
They turned down a network gig
when asked to lip-sync
perching on bales of hay.

Robbie flings out rhymes
to Richard's left-hand chords,

Levon yodels a melody —
no borders, no more "side men."
None of them says a word
when they land on the cover of *Time*.

VENGEROV'S VIOLIN

My violin was made in 1727. Moving at [contemporary] speeds
surprises it. It wants to go by boat. Or by train. In the time of
Mozart or Beethoven, life was different, slower.
— Maxim Vengerov

That bump
on the
horizon — sun?
Set? Risen?

Maine?
Seine?
The Red — no, the Irish
Sea —
Tokyo, Rio, Cape Town, Perth, Mumbai —
Missouri?

Even the clouds are speeding.
    Juggled, dizzy moons,
    promo'd orbits,
    flurries of tickets,
            green room, green room, green room —

Maxim! Let's get becalmed,
spend meandering weeks
in the Brahms.
Reverse-thrust through eons,
follow the aerial career
of at most three motes of dust.

.

This flipping clock counts milliseconds.
The tocker at the archduke's
stuck at one.
      Sails on lumbering brigs —
the tree that made me stood five hundred years.
I feel its still forest in my fibres.
I'd rather lurch forward in a howdah,
ride the balking apex of a snail.

I recall some outdoor fête:
a brackish pool,
the fish nearly snoring in the reeds;
their aimless, eddying schools. . . .

Or clattering to the *schloss*
over knobby cobbles
behind a stalling nag.
(That owner taught the lord's brat to sing.)
I was left on a gilded chair
by the footman's post.
A beetle spent all day clasping my strings.

THE WILDLIFE ILLUSTRATOR

House a dun bump on a ridge,
where winds on flaring jags
shove at the beardgrass, snag
on her eaves, could spin an oak
over the edge,

flip shingles off barns
like lottery cards — alone
at her diligent light,
she traces the torque
of a ram's corkscrew horn.

Trekkers of desert dark
arrive welcomed. Skinks flick
through a vent to her quilt.
She ferries one to an easel,
draws it for a county park.

Forgiven, javelinas test
her marigolds, again. At her door,
snakes reheat gelid hopes.
Beneath her straggling pear,
a roadrunner bustles to rest.

When thunder cracks the hills'
huddled backs, gunning for chimneys,
and winter lightning stabs —
strobes that once pinned
a neighbour's boy to her wall —

.

Powers, take note: through cactus weeks,
her paintbrushes caked,
she left on her simmering porch
a bucket brimming
where goldfinches dipped their beaks.

THE LATIN TEACHER

You tried to get our attention —
Puella, Puellae
who wanted for nothing,
drove cars worth more than your salary.
Analogues, declensions —

our culture's roots,
you'd said: word-provenance, *romanitas*,
plumbing. You showed us goatherds
mocking Senators' bromides
with homemade flutes.

We couldn't keep consuls straight,
which Gracchus brother did what.
A trading empire's daughters,
we wouldn't credit a seamstress
with spinning one's fate,

ignored dispatches from Gaul —
Caesar's blithe routs, the gore.
When we griped,
you pinned Seneca
to the Varsity wall.

Reciting next to the board
in your cracked flats
to slumping Anglo-Saxons
intent on Friday's dance,
you scooped from your hoard,

.

knobbed hands full of oblivion,
Horace's *ut doceat,*
Juvenal's guardian warning.
We crammed for tests at lunch
(*Doric? Corinthian?*),

thrilled to Pompeii's gold cache.
You pointed out the girl
who cradled her owner's child;
and the Greek slave's fresco,
up to the roof in ash.

IV

STATUE

You pose: bronze welded
to a bronzed plinth. Steel rods
prop soldered legs. That northward gaze
can track no amblers. Creases weight
stiff cuffs; your curls are nubs of lead.

Scoops in a passing cone
slant and wobble. Under your porkpie casque,
you watch shop-banners billow.
That concrete-trussed oak
can sway and groan.

To wake dizzy as a weathervane,
relish the tilt perspectives
of confetti; dwindle
to mere conduits for light
like florists' cellophane,

leap like a bebop tune's
jittery fourteenths, swerve
casually as a reconnoitering
beetle, migrate with
the knack of moons —

someone in the square has guessed your grief
and tied a gold balloon
to your locked hands
as though it could help you drift,
a sailfin tang through reef;

and has this raucous bird
been summoned? This child, hailing you?
Transfixed by gravities —
or fears, or fate — could
you be transformed by urgent words,

inch one creaking leg
into the air, heave off anvil boots,
bend down to her,
and ask to be
only as sturdy and promising as an egg?

Monotone conifer ranks.
Billboards flash sopped burger-domes,
stacked fries broad as planks.
Gasfume. Fume.
Fume. Truckstop looking
like it fell off a truck.
Commuter-radio drones.

Shift, curve — Ferris wheel
blinking over that wall?
Magenta strobing — squeals —
red aerial
speedboats veering. . . . Winged elephants
swoop past tents
where Fortune's wheels don't stall

under young travellers' weather:
cloudtufts drifting down
(white and pink spun sugar
floating on paper cones).
Over routes varied by tune,
new riders canter stallions
whose green hooves never strike ground.

ANTICLEA AND DAUGHTER

She clutches sunblock to aching knees, scanning
for any god with a kelp beard
who's whipped his speedboat too close,
squinting hard at the sea

where her daughter rides crests shoreward,
rowing the horizon. Anticlea
could ask the moon
to shuffle a tide,

or slit, like birthday ribbon, a thousand
jellyfish trains.
Each time her girl dives, Anticlea braces
for a scouting fin.

When, years on, the hurricane snatches
the boardwalk and the god
drowns carousel horses'
pink and blue manes,

briefly the daughter yearns
for the old cove —
then reefs the salt-caked storm-jib,
harvests her pears and honey.

Finally I found that pair!
Tossed in an old trunk,
salt streaking cracking soles,
their gold tongues parched —
decades since I'd worn them.
But I slipped them on, was there —

café where we'd just met:
sailing on our coffee,
whipped berets of cream;
the table tipped toward you.
Too shy to meet your eyes,
I shredded sugar packets.

Trucks spluttered by, panes shook,
staff started flipping the chairs,
we edged to the midnight street.
I couldn't believe my luck
when you said, "I'll need it soon"
and tossed me a dog-eared book.

These vagrant, flaking heels
clattered eight morning blocks
to class each week — up marble, down
granite steps; in the breeze
of subway-rush
knocked out a klutzy reel,

whacked the vending machine
in the basement stacks

till midnight. Popcorn
wedged in their treads
as we watched hatbrims nudge
in Bogie's tarmac scene,

and wandering a fog one dawn
(we'd missed the last bus back)
those boots on frosted sidewalks
played rhythm to pigeon-descant,
Orion switching off,
dorm-windows blinking on,

till we paused at your hall door.
We didn't wake till dusk.
From your arms I glimpsed
our coats flung on your desk,
my right boot, sideways, giddy,
paired with the left of yours.

THE FINDER

You've reconciled lost spouses
of earrings,
netted a shoe
that had taken to wandering the house.

Summoning fugitive keys
with magnetized fingers
or an invisible headlamp,
you take the hints of a breeze.

You block escape-routes
gently, almost as if
you're waiting open-armed
at the base of a laundry chute.

Cultures with furtive heels
return to your scholar's view,
whole biographies
lost on oxdrawn wheels;

memories in muddy pools
of past years resurface
if you cast at their edge,
cluster in eager schools.

Given such powers,
could you rescue
with a lighthouse-rake of dark waves
our foundered hours —

.

past the moldings' keep
retrieve for me
years of your midnight riffs,
soft words before sleep?

ANTICANCER CHARM

Shrink to light as a linseed grain,
no heftier than a handworm's hip;
vanish, vapor from sunshot pails.
Minimus, diminish. Dissolve
every bulwark. Strike your bad town.

TERMINAL

Blurred in porchlight-glare,
a beige one-inch propeller
slows — to a dangling
moth, paunch at her throat;
the spider casts its
line into freezing

      air, cinching
      silk around
      the moth's torso,
      looping the legs,
      mother swaddling
      a child, starts

binding a trembling
wing; the flyer writhes
into revolutions till
you can almost hear
the hum as her sawdust-flake
keeps the deathtrap

      shaking; whirls, thrusts,
      droops. . . . The spider
      scuttles, shackles the last
      free leg, circles
      her four times,
      five — now both wings

are trussed, the meal strung
at the web's heart,

antennae
lashed. The moth shoves
out her proboscis,
rampant, giving

tongue.

EXITS

Not skittering, puffs of lint.

Not dumped like spit —
with an absentminded flurry —
from Yahweh's trumpet.

Not marshalled before a clipboard
and a squint.

Let's breach a baleen foyer,
ride dark churning circles —

sprawl, briny, in wild lime — blinking
at parrot-aubades from palms.

LAST DAYS

in memory of Gabriele Helms, 1966–2004

My friend, you wouldn't lie down.
Your wandering IV pole
glided with you, loyal, rattling
on frantic circuits;
crisp pillows didn't tempt;
round, around, around, guppies

cruised the lobby tank,
flickering sunrise-slivers
all guts, mouths urging, urging;
tube-lights buzzed like bees
over your pale shoulders;
you wadded your pink gown, yanked

on crimson sweats
matching the bulbs you glimpsed
blazing that Christmas week
through nearby squares downtown; on
through the bluish hours
the night janitor's mop

swung drowsily over the lino,
the nurse tucked one leg up,
barely a monitor blinked;
scout in a cornered valley,
you looped your length of ground
as cancer hurtled to break

.

the bones that kept you pacing,
carrying your handsbreadth girl
(five-month spindle Buddha,
her brain's coral byways
travelled by your voice);
round, around, around, you

duelled to stay alive until
she could be born.
The doctors that last Tuesday
said it had to be now
and wheeled you off, upright.
Her shivering two red pounds —

you never got to cup them.
Did you hear her cry?
Three days later,
your gray eyes glazed,
blank. We stroked your hands.
What could wrench you down?

Your daughter's walking now;
we dash chasing after.
Round, around, around,
tentative, urgent stumbles. . . .
Someday we will tell her
you refused to lie down.

ITALIAN FIFTEENTH-CENTURY
DOUBLE WEDDING PORTRAIT
The Cloisters, New York

You face each other,
in front of a stone façade
and a *paysage moralisé*
crammed with symbols of charity and fidelity:
rabbit, falcon, unicorn, dog, pelican.
A terracotta town blurs on a hilltop, a teal bay
cradles five ships; someone poles a skiff up a creek.

The Latin on the frieze above you reads:
"So our features may survive."
(Hers: stubborn bump of a chin,
hooked nose; his: thick neck.)
Her auburn hair is wound with seedlike pearls;
a locket dangles against her ivory skin
and pine-green bodice. His red vest matches his cap.

No one's sure who you are.
You might be Matteo
di Sebastiano di Bernardino Gozzadini
and Ginevra d'Antonio Lupari —
the coat of arms suggests
two of Bologna's richest families
yoked near the Quattrocento's close.

The invisible sailors on the ships,
the hunters and fishermen
at the panel's edges
might have liked to pose
with this portrait's phoenix ("rebirth of a family line")

so history could also witness their pledges —
like Matteo offer a pink to Ginevra's orange.

Here in a land unknown
by Europe when this was painted,
the museum's night watchman
(no nametag) misses his fiancée.
When they marry next month, friends will snap photos
    with phones.
He has to dash before her workday begins,
to walk their pound-rescue mutt.

But tonight he's kept you,
Matteo and Ginevra, safe
through flashlit rounds,
like the artist whose brush kept you alive
five hundred years: maybe the Maestro delle Storie del Pane
(so-called by scholars; true name never found.
No coat of arms; probably Emilian-School).

GIFTS
to Steve

Yes, there are souvenirs —
holiday photos
posed at the waterfall or lumpy
dolmens, a mussed
napkin with a chocolate blotch,
pink palm-tree keychain;
the race-day T-shirt; inevitable postcards:
gargoyles, pillars, groves,
Sea World with a draped walrus.

But words invaluable
as a monkish scrip
overlooked by Calvinists;
a detail that snagged
on a log in a stream;
scenes bubbling toward me
from reservoirs —
all my memory-skiff
offers, then sails back to mist,

will vanish. I leave
nothing of enviable worth;
no children; tureens of cracked
china (an aunt's).
Why shouldn't I drift off
like a lost balloon?
But you gave me another gift:
"I'll carry you in my heart
till my last day on earth."

INVITATION
with thanks to Christopher Patton

The stag and doe
lift their heads
in the brush

ears raised
as if
attuned to our tears

The grass reaches through chairs
by the shed
as if to thatch cushions
for the pair of us

The gate that won't quite shut
with its scruff of lichen
invites us into the orchard

to pick "till time and times are done"
our choice of the bursting plums.

94

An endless fence
intervenes — millions of *i*- and
f-palings, beyond which lies
that imagined country:
Time and Funds Better Spent,

Roads That Might Have Been Taken,
Solace Freely Offered,
and, as always, Those
One Didn't Lose
Many Years Too Soon.

Burgees rippling, ships nudge in
for those who need them most —
no smokestacks loiter,
oblivious, taunt
from light horizons.

A niece doesn't die,
one massacre's forestalled.
Gifts never shrivel,
no one flails in the whirlpools
of a culture's lies.

We don't lose visas
in cabs; with the loves
of our lives,
we raid the warehouse
of inerrant fortune cookies.

.

— But the innumerable
trees ranged there
are the child's prototype,
birdsong vague as static;
nothing petite as a shell

on a wide-focus beach.
Still, we linger —
remedies that might have saved
loved hands, a town! Some globe
tender as a peach.

.

NOTES

Legacies — The verb "waked" here means "to give a wake for."

Astrolabe — This is a "found" poem, with all lines taken or slightly adapted from *Arabia Felix* by Thorkild Hansen (London: Collins, 1964).

Co-Education — "Bedder," an abbreviation of "bedmaker," is a term used at the University of Cambridge for the College housekeepers who since 1635 have cleaned faculty and student bedrooms.

Parish Dance — "Lady, by yonder blessèd moon I vow": William Shakespeare, *Romeo and Juliet,* II.ii.107, ed. G. Blakemore Evans (Cambridge: Cambridge University Press, 2003).

From a Niece — "our summer made her light escape" is a phrase from the poem by Emily Dickinson beginning "As imperceptibly as grief." Thomas H. Johnson, ed., *The Complete Poems of Emily Dickinson* (Boston: Little, Brown, 1960).

Citydwellers — "BK" stands for "Burger King."

Gettysburg, Field and Town — "Round Top" was a hill at Gettysburg where there was particularly fierce fighting. "Pickets" refers to soldiers acting as sentinels. Casualties at Gettysburg involved many amputations.

Collateral Damage — "Anything vertical to the horizon wants to fall. We're just helping it." — Doug Loizeaux, owner of a demolition business that popularized the term "implosion." The information about structures in stanza three is also taken from comments made by Loizeaux.

If Clouds Had Strings — Szabolcs Kéri, a psychologist at Semmelweis University in Hungary, and his researchers devised a test to determine volunteer subjects' creativity; the test used prompts like "What if clouds had strings?"

Big Pink — Nickname for a house (with pink siding) rented by several members of The Band (comprised of Canadians Rick Danko, Garth Hudson, Richard Manuel, Robbie Robertson, and American Levon Helm) in West Saugerties, New York. Here, in the basement, The Band composed much of their first studio album, *Music from Big Pink* (1968). In his autobiography, *This Wheel's on Fire*, Levon Helm implied that when The Band suddenly appeared on the cover of *Time* magazine (on January 12, 1970), none of the members were interested enough in this fact to mention it to each other.

Last Days — Gabriele Helms, a scholar of Canadian literature who emigrated to British Columbia from her native Germany, led the first conference in Canada for young women with breast cancer, which took place in June 2004. On December 31 of that year, she died of metastatic breast cancer, three days after giving birth to her only child.

Anticlea and Daughter — In Greek literature, Anticlea is Odysseus's mother.

Anticancer Charm —This poem adapts a translation by Richard Hamer of "A Charm," in his *A Choice of Anglo-Saxon Verse* (London: Faber and Faber, 1970).

Invitation —"Till time and times are done" is a phrase from the last stanza of William Butler Yeats's poem "The Song of Wandering Aengus." *The Collected Poems of W. B. Yeats* (New York: Macmillan, 1956).

ACKNOWLEDGEMENTS

This book was written with the assistance of grants from the Canada Council for the Arts and the British Columbia Arts Council, and a residency at the Virginia Center for the Creative Arts, which was subsidized by the National Endowment for the Arts. David O'Meara was an extraordinarily conscientious, intelligent, and generous editor, engaging in a dialogue with Elise over a number of months and devoting equal care to several successive versions of many poems. Barbara Nickel and Christopher Patton similarly gave the entire manuscript sustained, patient, and prompt attention. Robert Pinsky also read the manuscript and made valuable suggestions for improvement. Anne Balant-Campbell read many poems aloud to Elise and offered crucial advice. Damian Rogers, Kelly Joseph, and Cindy Ma of Anansi managed the book's editing, production, and entry into the world with the greatest sympathy. Peter Norman's copyediting and Stuart Ross's proofreading were meticulous. Elise was especially pleased by the openness of Anansi and Brian Morgan to her request that the cover design incorporate a painting by her former teacher and lifelong friend Ruth K. Fackenthal. To the many people who offered Elise love and support through the difficult months during which this book was being completed—of whom there is room here to name only her brother, Tim Tompkins— Elise was, and I shall always remain, infinitely grateful.

S.P.

The following poems have been previously published, sometimes in different forms:

Arc: "Legacies," "Parish Dance," "Range"

The Baffler: "Placard at the Los Angeles Excavation Site, 5002 A.D."

PN Review: "Litany," "Waltzing"

PRISM international: "The Alphabet," "Before the Fall," "If Clouds Had Strings"

Slate: "Last Days"

Southwest Review: "From a Niece"

The Walrus: "The Finder," "A Late Writer's Desk," "Then"

Winnipeg Review: "Alternate Histories," "Co-Education," "Domestic Interior: Child Watching Mother"

Yale Review: "Vengerov's Violin"

Elise Partridge's *Fielder's Choice* was shortlisted for the Gerald Lampert Award for best first book of poems in Canada; her *Chameleon Hours* was a finalist for the BC Book Prize, won the Canadian Authors Association Poetry Award, and was featured in the *Washington Post* "Poet's Choice" column. Her work has been anthologized in Canada, the U.S., Ireland, and the U.K., and has appeared in *Arc, Poetry, The Walrus, The New Yorker, The Fiddlehead, Slate, PN Review, Poetry Ireland Review, Southwest Review, Yale Review,* and *The New Republic.*